MARTIN HEIDEGGER

MAKERS OF CONTEMPORARY THEOLOGY

EDITORS:

The Rev. Professor D. E. NINEHAM
The Rev. E. H. ROBERTSON

PAUL TILLICH, *by J. Heywood Thomas*
RUDOLF BULTMANN, *by Ian Henderson*
DIETRICH BONHOEFFER, *by E. H. Robertson*
TEILHARD DE CHARDIN, *by Bernard Towers*
MARTIN BUBER, *by Ronald Gregor Smith*
GABRIEL MARCEL, *by Sam Keen*
LUDWIG WITTGENSTEIN, *by W. D. Hudson*
MARTIN HEIDEGGER, *by John Macquarrie*
SØREN KIERKEGAARD, *by Robert L. Perkins*
ALFRED NORTH WHITEHEAD, *by Norman Pittenger*
FRIEDRICH SCHLEIERMACHER, *by Stephen Sykes*

MARTIN HEIDEGGER

by

JOHN MACQUARRIE

JOHN KNOX PRESS
RICHMOND, VIRGINIA

British edition published by the Lutterworth Press
4 Bouverie Street, London, England, 1968

American edition published by John Knox Press,
Richmond, Virginia, 1968

International Standard Book Number: 0-8042-0659-7
Library of Congress Catalog Card Number: 68-11970

First published 1968
Fourth printing 1973

TO
IAN HENDERSON

Printed in the U.S.A.

Contents

Preface

It may seem strange to include Martin Heidegger in a series of books dealing with "Makers of Contemporary Theology", for Heidegger is no theologian but a philosopher, and he is often reckoned to be a thoroughly secular philosopher at that. Yet I think it would be true to say that one could hardly hope to advance very far in the understanding of contemporary theology without some knowledge of Heidegger's thought. His influence seems to appear everywhere—in demythologizing and the problem of hermeneutics; in the doctrine of man; in theories of revelation; in the debate about God; and in other matters besides. Though not himself a theologian, he is a maker of theology, in the same way in which Plato and Aristotle and Kant have been makers of theology. So we make no excuse for including him in this series. Heidegger's philosophy is no substitute for Christian theology, and certainly it should not be allowed to dominate the work of the theologian, but it does provide the kind of conceptual framework that the theologian needs if he is to state the Christian faith in terms intelligible to today's world.

John Macquarrie.

Union Theological Seminary,
New York City,
April, 1967.

I

Life

B Y any standard, Martin Heidegger must be reckoned among the greatest and most creative philosophers of the twentieth century. His influence has spread far beyond his own discipline. As well as philosophers, there must be counted theologians, psychotherapists, historiographers and many others, who have gained insights from Heidegger's work and applied them to their own tasks.

Heidegger was born at Messkirch, Baden, in 1889. Thus his background is the countryside of south-west Germany and the life of the agricultural community. However subtle and sophisticated his philosophy may have become, something of this simpler early way of life remains. Heidegger's philosophy has retained a kind of earthiness, that prevents him from flying off into distant realms of speculation, as so many German sages have done. It may have been his country background that enabled him to keep an interest in poetry, at a time when appreciation for poetry has become largely atrophied. Heidegger's origins may also have helped him to maintain his independent, critical and almost prophetic stance in the technological age, for although he is so much a man of the twentieth century, he has not permitted himself to become simply the captive of his own age or to be dazzled by its achievements. Above all, he has been aware of some of the dangers that, in a mass society, threaten the simple freedoms and dignities of human life and can make it something less than human.

At first attracted to the priesthood, Heidegger studied for a time in a Jesuit seminary. He decided, however, that his vocation lay in philosophy, so he left. But he still acknowledges that his work in the seminary made its contribution to the development of his thought, and especially that it awakened his interest in hermeneutics and language. His philosophical studies took place at the University of Freiburg, where the bright star in those days was Edmund Husserl. It was from Husserl that Heidegger learned the phenomenological method, though he adapted it to his own purposes. His permanent debt to Husserl was acknowledged when he dedicated his own major work, *Sein und Zeit*, to his old teacher. Already, however, another influence was working on Heidegger. When he was eighteen, he had read Franz Brentano's book, *Von der mannigfachen Bedeutung des Seienden bei Aristoteles*—a treatise on the meanings of "being" in Aristotle. This reading awakened in Heidegger the quest that has dominated his whole philosophical career—the quest for the meaning of "being".

His first chair was at the University of Marburg, and it was during his professorship there that he published *Sein und Zeit* in 1927. This work immediately put him among the foremost philosophers of the day. We may also recall that at Marburg he had among his colleagues two of the great Protestant theologians of the twentieth century—Rudolf Bultmann and Paul Tillich.

In 1928 he returned to the University of Freiburg. He created a sensation by his famous inaugural lecture, in which he dealt with "nothing", as the theme of metaphysics. The remainder of his teaching and writing career has been lived out in or near Freiburg, in the Black Forest country to which he belongs.

Soon after Heidegger went to Freiburg, Germany began to experience troubled times as the new National Socialist Party began to make its influence felt. Though there seems to be little in his philosophy that would be sympathetic to the fantastic pseudo-philosophy of such Nazi "intellectuals" as Alfred Rosenberg, Heidegger, like many other Germans, joined the party in the belief that it offered the best hope for the renewal of the nation. There has been much controversy over the question of his relation to the Nazi régime. The party certainly tried to exploit the advantage of having so illustrious a member, and soon after Hitler came to power, Heidegger became Rector of the University. In his official capacity, he identified himself with the policies of the government. Some of Heidegger's opponents have made as much as possible of his Nazi connections, in attempts (sometimes quite unscrupulous) to discredit him. However, a study of his speeches and writings during the time of his Rectorship shows that although he was a firm supporter of the party, he did not share in its fanatical excesses. In any case, he very soon became disillusioned. He gave up the Rectorship and his favourable mentions of the régime ceased. His defenders praise his actions at this time, and claim that he left the party at a juncture when it was extremely difficult to do so.

But after the end of World War II, Heidegger was not *persona grata* in the new Germany. He now spent much of his time writing at his retreat in the Black Forest, occasionally coming in to Freiburg in order to give a lecture. Meantime, his fame had become worldwide, and people from many countries came to visit him at his mountain home.

Plans have been made for the translation into English of the entire body of Heidegger's writings. At the time when this book is being written, the following works of Heidegger have appeared in translation (German titles and original publication dates are shown in brackets) : *An Introduction to Metaphysics*, 1959 (*Einführung in die Metaphysik*, 1953); *Kant and the Problem of Metaphysics*, 1962 (*Kant und das Problem der Metaphysik*, 1929); *Being and Time*, 1962 (*Sein und Zeit*, 1927); *Discourse on Thinking*, 1966 (*Gelassenheit*, 1959). In addition, several essays and shorter pieces have been translated. Already there has been in the English-speaking world, and especially in the United States, a remarkable surge of interest in Heidegger's work, and this interest is likely to grow as more of his writings are translated.

2

Thought

Being and Existence

HEIDEGGER'S philosophy is concerned with the question of the meaning of Being.[1] This was indeed the question which stirred the early researches of Western philosophy. But it is now a question that has fallen into neglect or is even regarded as a pseudo-question. It is true that we can hardly utter two sentences without using some part of the verb "to be", and one might almost say that this verb, whether expressed or understood, holds our discourse together. We do indeed speak of "is" as the copula. Yet analytical philosophers in particular are highly suspicious of any inquiry into Being (especially when this is spelled with a capital letter!) Their nominalism leads them to suppose that anyone engaging in such an inquiry (ontology) has fallen into the error of supposing that because we have a noun "Being" in the language, there must be some thing corresponding to the word, out there in the world.

As a matter of fact, Heidegger has always been quite clear in his mind that Being, however we are to think of it, cannot be considered as a thing, another entity or something that is. His philosophy is perhaps the most consistent attempt up till now to break away from the traditional domination of Western thought by the category of substance (thinghood), and this is one aspect of his thought that makes it so excitingly new and important for the modern world. He is careful never to formulate the question of the meaning of Being in the form "What is

[1] The word "Being" (capitalized) will be used to translate *das Sein*; the German expression *das Seiende*, "that which is", will be variously translated as "being" (lower case) or "entity".

Being? ", for to ask this question would be to imply that Being "is" a "what", a thing or substance or entity.

But he recognizes that the prevailing climate of thought is not favourable to the question of Being, and that if this question is to be heard again, some prejudices must be overcome. He mentions[2] three common prejudices that militate against an intelligent interest in the question about the meaning of Being. The first prejudice is that "Being" is the most universal of concepts, for whatever we think about, we think of it as something that is. But "Being" is not a property or class-concept like "redness". If it were, it would indeed be an almost completely vacuous notion, so that to inquire into it would be a waste of time. The word "Being" does not designate a class but lies beyond all distinctions of classes. This was already seen by Aristotle, and also in medieval ontology, where "Being" was reckoned a *transcendens*, because it does not fall under any of the ordinary categories of thought. A second prejudice follows from the first. It is supposed that "Being" is indefinable. This would be true if definitions must be given by naming the class (genus) and specific difference of that which is to be defined, and obviously this would be impossible if "Being" were understood as the most universal class-concept. But we have already seen that "Being" cannot be regarded as a class or universal property. So the fact that it cannot be defined by this rather old-fashioned method of definition does not imply that there is no problem here. It simply indicates again that 'Being' cannot be understood as another entity that might be defined in the conventional manner, and drives us to ask how we can look for a way of discussing the meaning of "Being". Finally, there is the prejudice that "Being" is a self-evident concept. Once more, there is some truth in this, for we continually use the verb "to be", and so we must have some understanding of it. But if we are asked about the meaning, we find that it becomes very elusive. As Heidegger understands the matter, the business

[2] *Being and Time*, tr. J. Macquarrie and E. S. Robinson (SCM, London; Harper, New York, 1962), pp. 22-3.

of the philosopher is to investigate some of these dimly understood notions that we already have, such as this notion of
"Being" of which we make constant use, and to clarify them
and bring them into the light of day, rather than just say they
are "self-evident".

To ask a question about anything seems to imply both that
we already have some understanding, however dim, of what we
are asking about, and yet at the same time that we lack an
understanding of it. For every question has already some
direction, and we could hardly ask about anything unless we
had at least some idea of what we were asking about; yet we would
not trouble to ask about anything unless it were something
that we did not know about. These remarks are obviously true
about the question of Being. The very fact that we continually
use the verb "to be" shows that from the outset we already
stand in an understanding of what it means to be, and yet this
understanding, when we are challenged to say what it is, turns
out to be very vague and difficult to pin down. So perhaps the
answer to the question about the meaning of Being is to be
reached simply through a process of clarifying and conceptu-
alizing that vague indefinite understanding that we all already
have.

This suggestion is confirmed when we analyse further the
question of Being. If we inquire about anything whatsoever, we
have to select and examine such data as will yield an understanding of what we are inquiring about. If we are inquiring
about Being, then our data would seem the things that are, the
particular beings which may be said to manifest or exemplify
Being. But there is an infinite range of such beings—atoms,
mountains, trees, stars; anything of which it can be said that it
is, is a being. Is there any particular being that is specially
qualified to serve as the starting-point for an inquiry into Being
in general? Heidegger thinks that there is. The particular
being that has to be interrogated with respect to its own
"is-hood" is the questioner himself. Like the atoms, mountains,
trees, stars and any other entities we may care to mention, man

is ; but he differs from all these others because he not only is, but has an understanding of what it means "to be". Within limits, indeed, he is responsible for what he is. As Heidegger often says, his Being is an issue for him.[3] Because man has a measure of openness, of freedom and responsibility, the question of who he is, is inescapable for him ; but this question, if pursued in a radical way, leads with equal inescapability into the question of Being in general.

In effect, Heidegger is saying that man is the ontological entity. This does not mean, of course, that everyone pursues philosophical ontology (the explicit inquiry into Being) ; but it does mean that from the very way man is constituted, he cannot help coming to some decisions, even if these are only implicit in the way he lives, about the Being that is already an issue for him in the very way he *is*. Concerning the ontological question, Heidegger remarks : "Each of us is grazed at least once, perhaps more than once, by the hidden power of this question, even if he is not aware of what is happening to him".[4]

When he talks about man, Heidegger generally employs the German expression *Dasein* to draw attention to man's ontological constitution. This German expression is usually left untranslated in English discussions of Heidegger's thought. Literally, it means "Being-there", though in traditional German philosophy it was used in the sense of "existence". To say that man is "Being-there" calls attention to his finitude, as the one who always finds himself in a particular situation ; at the same time, he is "there" in the sense that his "there" is disclosed to him and is his centre of reference. Although *Dasein* was traditionally used for "existence" generally, Heidegger restricts it to human existence, and this very word "existence" is also used in a restricted sense for the kind of Being that belongs to *Dasein*. We have already noticed that while man, atoms, mountains, trees, stars, and innumerable things besides, all *are*, man is

---

[3] Cf. *Being and Time*, p. 236.
[4] *An Introduction to Metaphysics*, **tr.** Ralph Manheim (Yale University Press, New Haven, 1959), p.1.

distinguished from all the rest because he not only *is*, but has some understanding of and some responsibility for who he is. In this sense, he alone "exists", that is to say, he "stands out" (ex-sists) from the general run of beings as the particular being who has to decide about Being. "*Dasein* is a being for which, in its Being, that Being is an issue."[5] In restricting the expression "existence" to *Dasein*, Heidegger is not for a moment denying reality to atoms, mountains, trees, stars and the rest. These are real enough, but they do not have the kind of Being that lets them "stand out" in the peculiar sense of "existing".

Heidegger is often called an "existentialist", and certainly his philosophy is existentially based. The quest for Being begins from the Being of the questioner himself, the human *Dasein*, and proceeds to unfold the structure of his existence. But Heidegger is not an existentialist in the narrow sense of one whose primary interest is in man, or one who makes man's subjectivity the measure of all things. Although man is the exemplary being that is to be interrogated with respect to its Being so as to get the inquiry into Being off the ground, so to speak, Heidegger regards this task of exploring man's Being as "fundamental ontology", rather than as a self-contained study of man. From first to last, the goal toward which Heidegger's thought is thrusting is the question of the meaning of Being, in the widest sense.

There is a good deal of discussion about the relation of Heidegger's earlier work to his later work.[6] The earlier work is existential, in the sense that it is dominated by discussions of human existence, and these are expected to furnish the clues that will lead into the understanding of the meaning of Being. The later work is ontological, in the sense that it is dominated by a more direct confrontation with the idea of Being, and human existence is now understood in the light of Being. The difference between the two styles of philosophizing is sometimes so sharp

---

[5] *Being and Time*, p. 236.
[6] Cf. the present writer's article, "Heidegger's Earlier and Later Work Compared", in *Anglican Theological Review*, vol. xlix, (1967), pp. 3-16.

that some commentators talk of the earlier and later Heideggers almost as if these were distinct persons with only loosely related philosophies !

That there is a "turning" in the development of Heidegger's thought, and that this turning is from a phase dominated by the notion of existence to another dominated by the notion of Being, is undeniable. But too much should not be made of it. The quest for Being remains constant throughout Heidegger's philosophy, and certainly he himself believes that there is a unity that holds together his work. This becomes particularly apparent in these later writings when he frequently interprets his earlier utterances in line with his most recent thought.

We can best understand the relation of the earlier and the later work, and likewise the successive dominance of the ideas of existence and Being, in terms of a massive dialectic. The focus of the inquiry is always the question of the meaning of Being. But there is no straightforward or simple path that leads to the solution of this problem. One must first come at it from the side of man's existence and from his firsthand understanding of what it means to be in the world ; but then one must come back to look afresh at human existence in the light of whatever understanding can be gained of that wider Being within the context of which our human existence is set.

The structure of this dialectic was already sketched out by Heidegger in the opening pages of *Being and Time*.[7] There he draws attention to what he calls the "hermeneutical circle". This is not to be understood like the "circular reasoning" that begs the question. It is rather a "relatedness backward or forward" that is present in every act of interpretation, for interpretation could get started only if we already had some understanding of what is to be interpreted, whilst there would be no point in any interpretation unless our initial understanding were filled out, corrected and perhaps very much altered in the course of the interpretation. The understanding of Being which

[7] See pp. 27-8.

B

is already given with human existence, as itself a kind of Being, allows the inquiry to get started; but finally existence itself can be understood only in the light of Being.

Thus the dialectic between existence and Being, the existential and the ontological, is set up at an early stage in Heidegger's thought. Those who complain that they cannot see how the earlier and later work are related have become bogged down in details so that they fail to perceive the vast strategy that unifies Heidegger's philosophy.

The Existential Analytic

We have seen that the inquiry into Being is to take its departure from an examination of the particular being that raises the question of Being, namely, from *Dasein* or the human existent. The question of Being, therefore, is to be approached by way of the question of existence, the kind of Being that belongs to *Dasein*. Because every *Dasein* has to be, and has to decide about its own existence and to understand itself in one way or another, then every *Dasein* is already involved in the question of existence in a very concrete way. This concrete, inescapable question which everyone has concerning how he is to understand and decide about his own existence is called by Heidegger the "existentiell" question. This is to be distinguished from the "existential" question, which is an explicit theoretical inquiry into the structures of existence generally. While everybody is faced with the existentiell question of deciding about his own existence, only a few philosophers raise the explicitly existential question and reflect on the basic constitution of human existence as such. But the existential question is rooted in the existentiell one, that is to say, the theoretical inquiry takes its rise from the concrete situation of existing in the world. Heidegger shares the common existentialist distrust of abstract rationalism. The question of Being is not to be considered in terms of abstract speculation, but on the basis of our own firsthand participation in existence. Men are not spectators of Being but participants in it, and if there is to be a philosophy of Being, this cannot be reared on any kind of detached observation, but only on the basis of our total participation.

What is to be done then is to set forth the basic structures of human existence as these are disclosed to us in our own existing. This task of mapping out the constitution of the *Dasein* is called by Heidegger the "existential analytic". It is an attempt to lay bare the "existentiality" of existence, that is to say, the core of distinctive characteristics that mark off the existent from other kinds of beings.

The method of the existential analytic is phenomenological. One might say that the essence of phenomenology is careful, analytic description. Heidegger's exposition of phenomenology[8] proceeds by one of his favourite methods, that is to say, by a discussion of the etymology of the word "phenomenology" itself. He discusses first the "phenomenon", that which "shows itself" or "lets itself be seen" for what it is ; then he turns to the "logos", which, as speech, is also a "showing". Thus phenomenology is fundamentally a showing of that which shows itself, a stripping away of concealments and distortions, such as will let us see that which lets itself be seen for what it is. In Quentin Lauer's words, "The phenomenological method . . . is not one of "proof" ; rather, it is one of description, wherein it is *hoped* that others will see things the same way".[9] Although the allusion here is to Husserl rather than to Heidegger, the remark would hold for both of these philosophers. Heidegger's existential analytic does in fact consist of detailed descriptions of some basic characteristics of human existence, and the test of his descriptions is to compare them with what we ourselves actually know of existence through our own firsthand participation in it.

Yet to furnish and to test a description of the basic structures

---

[8] *Being and Time*, pp. 49-61.
[9] *Phenomenology: its Genesis and Prospect* (Harper & Row, New York, 1965), p. 84.

of existence is not nearly so simple a matter as it may sound when first mentioned. Existence is not an object that we can set before us and describe from the outside, as it were. We ourselves are the existents that are to be described, and self-knowledge is notoriously difficult. Perhaps the existent has even a tendency to conceal what he really is, and so we find Heidegger saying that the phenomena have to be wrested from the tendencies that cover them up, and are certainly not just to be read off by an unreflective beholder. Furthermore, what are we to say about the individual differences between one person and another? Could there be an analysis of existence that was valid for everyone?

Thus, before we plunge into Heidegger's actual analyses, we must think a little more about the enterprise of an existential analytic. Can we see more clearly how such an inquiry might proceed, and what results it might hope to reach?

Perhaps these questions can best be answered by taking a closer look at the concept of existence. It has already been pointed out [10] that Heidegger does not use the word "existence" in its traditional sense but restricts it to the kind of Being that belongs to *Dasein*, the human existent. He stands out ("ex-sists") in the sense that he is not just another item in the world, but a being open to himself and open to his world so that, within limits, he has responsibility for both of these and can shape them to some extent. What is distinctive in the concept of existence may be seen if we contrast the "existent" with the other beings which are found within the world—beings that are just as real as *Dasein*, but which do not "exist" in the sense of the word employed by Heidegger and existentialist philosophers generally.

(*a*) *Dasein* is never complete in its Being. To exist is always to be on the way, so that one can never, as it were, pin down the existent at any precise moment and give an exhaustive description. He is constituted by possibilities rather than

[10] See above, p. 7

properties. Other beings have "essences" that are more or less
fixed, and given to them. A piece of rock, for instance, can be
fairly adequately described by listing such properties as its
colour, hardness, chemical composition and the like. But
Dasein has no fixed essence of this kind. So far as we can talk
about his "essence" at all, we would have to say that he makes
it as he goes along, fulfilling his possibilities or letting them
slip, but always on the move from one situation to the next.
This is what is meant by saying that "the essence of *Dasein* lies
in its existence".[11] Thus the existential analytic will not describe
universal "properties", but simply possible ways in which the
Dasein may exist. These possible ways of existing, Heidegger
calls the *existentialia*. These may be compared (and likewise
contrasted) with the traditional "categories", the most general
concepts used for describing beings other than *Dasein*.

(*b*) The existence of *Dasein* is characterized in every case by a
unique "mineness"; it is always someone's own existence.
This unique individuality of the *Dasein* is hard to express
precisely, but we recognize it in our ordinary experience. It is a
matter of indifference which particular copy of the morning
newspaper I get, for they are all alike, and to have read one is to
have read the lot. But one *Dasein* cannot be substituted for
another as a matter of indifference. The *Dasein* is addressed by a
personal pronoun. The *Dasein* is not just a specimen of a class
of beings. To some extent, these remarks all flow from the point
made above, that *Dasein* does not have a fixed essence given to
it, or that its existence precedes its essence. But if the *Dasein*
cannot be treated as a specimen of a class, how then is anything
like an existential analytic possible ? We have already seen that
the existential analytic will not describe universally occurring
properties. But it is possible to visualize a description of the
horizons of possibility (that is to say, the existential possibilities)
within which the concrete (existentiell) possibilities of any
actual *Dasein* would fall.

[11] *Being and Time*, p. 67.

(*c*) A *Dasein* can either choose itself or lose itself; it can either exist (stand out) as the distinctive being which it is, or it can be submerged in a kind of anonymous routine manner of life, in which its possibilities are taken over and dictated to it by circumstances or by social pressures. Thus there are two fundamental modes of existence : *authentic* existence, in which *Dasein* has taken possession of its own possibilities of Being, and *inauthentic* existence, in which these possibilities have been relinquished or suppressed. Presumably each individual *Dasein* exists for much of its time in an inauthentic way, and certainly authenticity is not something that can be gained once for all, but must be decided for in new situations as they come along.

The existential analytic has the task of filling out in detail the schematic concept of existence, as we have outlined it in the last few paragraphs. Heidegger begins with what he calls "everyday" existence, the kind that lies nearest to hand but the kind that is also most routine and most likely to be inauthentic. From there, he goes on to describe the authentic style of existing, as it breaks out beyond the everyday. We shall follow his order, and begin by considering everyday existence.

Everyday Being-in-the-world

Dasein is always in a world, and Heidegger talks of "Being-in-the-world" as the basic constitutive state of *Dasein*.[12] Thus the *Dasein* is considered in concrete, embodied existence, and not as a bare thinking subject. Heidegger does not waste time trying to prove that there is a real external world. Such a proof would be required only if one began from the erroneous idea that man is primarily a thinking subject. But man is inconceivable without a world to which he already stands in relation. The *Dasein* is from the beginning Being-in-the-world.

It is this hyphenated expression, Being-in-the-world, that

[1] Op. cit., p. 78ff.

also determines the shape of the existential analytic, at least in its initial stages. Although Being-in-the-world is a unity, we can distinguish three factors that go to constitute it. The first is the notion of "Being-in"; what kind of relation is this? Next, there is the notion of the world; what is this environment or context in which existence is set? Finally, there is the question of the self; what does it mean to be a self, constituted by Being-in-the-world?

We begin with Heidegger's explanation of Being-in, though for the present this explanation is provisional only and will have to be expanded later. The point he makes is that when we talk about "Being-in-the-world", we have in mind a much richer relation than merely the spatial one of being located in the world. As we can see from such expressions as "He is in love" or "He was in the conspiracy", the preposition "in", when used of personal subjects, is not limited to spatial relations, as it is when we say "There is water in the glass". This wider kind of personal or existential "inhood" implies the whole relation of "dwelling" in a place. We are not simply located there, but are bound to it by all the ties of work, interest, affection and so on.

The "Being-in" which characterizes our everyday relation to the world is called by Heidegger "concern". This word covers all the ways in which we relate ourselves to our environment—producing, constructing, enjoying and so forth. This fundamental kind of Being-in is therefore very practical. The relatively detached and theoretical relation to the world that is developed in the sciences is a derivative and highly specialized kind of understanding, attained by dimming down the element of practical concern so that we approach the point at which we simply behold or observe the world.

How then are we to understand the concept of "world" itself? Heidegger approaches this problem by considering how we understand any particular object within the world. Let us suppose, for instance, that we are confronted with a mountain. There are at least two ways in which we can think of it. We may think of it as just something lying around, something we have come across in the world ; in this case, the mountain is, in Heidegger's language, merely "present-at-hand". We are related to it only in a minimal kind of way, and it is not fully incorporated into our world. But we can also think of the mountain in relation to our practical concerns—as a quarry which can yield building material, as a recreation area which can serve for winter sports, as a look-out post, and in dozens of other ways. Now the mountain has become "ready-to-hand" and has become an item within the domain of practical concern.

The everyday world is therefore articulated in terms of the *Dasein's* practical concerns. Each item in it is understood as an instrument which can be used for the furthering and satisfaction of these concerns. But there is no such thing as an isolated instrument. Each instrument has its meaning only within a context of tasks, and these tasks are themselves all interlocking. Every instrument implies a whole series of others, and eventually the whole instrumental system that practical human concerns have built up. For the most part, we take this system for granted. We only become aware of it when something goes wrong. For instance, when there is a power failure, we suddenly realize how complex and interdependent is the man-made world in which we live.

Thus the world is understood by Heidegger as a vast instrumental system, held together, as it were, by *Dasein's* concern. It is in terms of this concern that things receive their significance, as they are incorporated into the world of man. In a similar fashion, space gets organized into a system of "places"—we become acutely aware of this when, for instance, we have moved into a new house and to begin with can no longer find anything in its place. Even time gets organized in terms of our practical concerns—a time to get up, a time to begin work, a time to eat, and so on.

In some respects, this philosophical theory of the world might seem rather appropriate to the technological age, for man is in fact transforming the merely natural world into a world that is increasingly man-made and in which everything is considered as ready-to-hand in relation to human concerns. Even what is left of nature becomes a park, serving the purpose of recreation.

However, we have to remember that Heidegger is talking of the *everyday* world, the world of routine tasks and conventional ways. As we shall soon see, he considers that we can easily lose ourselves in such a world, and in an authentic existence, man is open to dimensions of the world beyond the merely instrumental understanding of it.

We now turn to the question of the "who" of *Dasein*. What are we to say of the self that is constituted by Being-in-the-world ?

It might be supposed that the question of the self had already been answered in our preliminary discussion of existence, when it was said that to exist is to "stand out" as the unique and distinctive being that is always mine and that expresses itself by the personal pronoun "I".[13] But we remember also that precisely in that discussion it was said that existence might be either authentic or inauthentic. Is true selfhood really disclosed in everyday existing, or is this for the most part an inauthentic existence ? "It could be that the 'who' of everyday *Dasein* just is *not* the 'I myself' ".[14]

Actually, Heidegger does think that for the most part authentic selfhood gets suppressed in everyday Being-in-the-world. The *Dasein*, though it has indeed constructed the world of its concern, becomes absorbed in that world. It tends itself to become part of the system, to be caught up in the processes which it has itself originated, to become just another part of the machinery. This is an ironical destiny, yet it is one that has overtaken millions of people in industrial societies. Incidentally, it seems to be of such industrial societies that Heidegger is chiefly thinking, and it is not so clear how some of his analyses would apply either to the pre-industrial rural societies with their simpler but perhaps more exacting work-patterns, or to

[13] See above, p. 13
[14] *Being and Time*, p. 150.

the automated societies of the future with their possibilities for unprecedented leisure.

But the main reasons for Heidegger's estimate of everyday existence lie elsewhere, and are independent of the above considerations. The instrumental world is a common world. We encounter in it not only the things which we use, but also other people. Just as he did not waste time trying to prove the existence of an external world, Heidegger does not trouble to prove that there are other selves. On the contrary, he holds that community or "Being-with" is a basic *existentiale* of the *Dasein*. Just as there is no existence apart from a world, so there is no existence apart from other existents. But the other existent is not seen as an object within the world but as a *co-Dasein*. Thus we are related to the other existent not in terms of the "concern" (handling, producing and the like) by which we relate to things, but in terms of a personal concern or "solicitude" that characterizes relations between selves.

An authentic solicitude for the other helps him to his freedom and to his own unique possibilities for selfhood. But more often the relation to the other is one of indifference or is even an attempt to dominate him and to take his distinctive existence from him. In particular, the individual falls under the domination of the collective mass. His standards and his whole way of life are set for him by the conventions of his society. To choose possibilities is what belongs distinctively to existing, but the possibilities of choice are taken away. Especially in the mass societies of the contemporary world, with their mass-products and mass-media of communication and entertainment, a kind of drab uniformity and conformism is imposed upon all. Yet if we ask who it is, that has done this, it is impossible to identify anyone in particular. The indefinite, anonymous "they" have done it—*das Man*, in Heidegger's expression. "They" are pushing ahead with the armaments race ; "they" are spending billions on space exploration ; "they" are saying that . . . In all this, there is no genuine communication and no authentic Being-with-one-another.

"The self of everyday *Dasein*," declares Heidegger, "is the 'they-self', which we distinguish from the authentic self—that is, from the self that has been taken hold of in its own way."[15]

A Further Explication of Being-in-the-world

We have completed, as it were, the first round of the existential analytic, but much still remains in need of fuller explication. In particular, following Heidegger, we gave only a brief provisional account of Being-in, and this relation must now be examined in more detail, for clearly it is of paramount importance for the existential analytic. It is because of the peculiar way in which he is related to the world, his "Being-in" or "dwelling", that man "exists" and is distinct from entities that are simply within-the-world as parts of it. Man—or, more strictly, the *Dasein*—is Being-in-the-world, but his Being-in is such that it is also a standing-out (ex-sistence) ; in his awareness and responsibility, he has an openness to the world and a certain transcendence of the world.

Heidegger does not develop an epistemology in the traditional sense. He explicitly rejects such a task when he denies that *Dasein* is a thinking subject that somehow has to "go out" and relate itself to a world of objects. He begins instead, as we have seen, with Being-in-the-world, a concrete and many sided relation, of which theoretical knowledge is a derivative and abstract mode.[16] But even if we begin with man and the world together in concrete Being-in-the-world, the investigation of the kind of openness that belongs to Being-in would constitute a task something like the epistemology of older philosophies. Granting that we are already in the world and that our first-hand understanding of it comes by way of participation, striving, practical concern rather than theoretical observation, we still have to inquire into this openness, which is indeed what

[15] Op. cit., p. 167.
[16] See above, p. 15

distinguishes *Dasein* from all the other entities that we know. Heidegger can say : "*Dasein* is its disclosedness".[17] *Dasein* he can also describe as a clearing, like an open place in a forest where the light gets through. He talks often too of the "transparency" of *Dasein*. He sees all of these ideas as related to the traditional doctrine of a "natural light" in man. It is this "natural light" or "clearness" of Being-in-the-world that Heidegger proceeds to investigate. He holds that Being-in-the-world is disclosed to itself in two basic and equally primordial ways—through the affects and through understanding.

He considers first the affective states which, at any given time, colour our experience. Such states Heidegger regards as constituting a fundamental *existentiale*. They light up "the way we find ourselves". Ordinarily, these states of mind are regarded simply as moods, elusive and fugitive feelings that come and go, and certainly of no philosophical interest. Yet in Heidegger's view these moods may light up our Being-in-the-world in very fundamental ways. A mood reveals how we are attuned to our environment. It is not just a subjective emotion but an appreciation from the inside, as it were, of the situation in which we find ourselves. The mode of apprehension in such affective states is neither objective nor subjective, but rather comes before the separation of subject and object. It belongs to the totality of our "being there", and it lights up the "there" for us.

As examples of the affective states of which he is speaking, Heidegger mentions in various places fear, joy, boredom and anxiety. As we shall see in due course, a special significance attaches to anxiety. But all of these states of mind light up the situation in which we find ourselves.

The expression which Heidegger uses to characterize the disclosure that comes in affective states is "facticity". This does not and cannot mean that *Dasein* is just another fact in the world. In saying that *Dasein's* mode of Being is existence,

---

[17] *Being and Time*, p. 171.

Heidegger has already implied that *Dasein* is not another object in the world, not just another fact of which account must be taken. By "facticity" is meant that the *Dasein* always finds itself in a situation where it has "to be". It never begins with wide open horizons, so to speak, for at any moment there are already a great many "givens". Some of these may have arisen from the *Dasein's* own past choices, but there will be others that it has not chosen at all, and that will have been determined for it by society or history or heredity or other agencies. Up till now we have talked of the existent primarily in terms of possibility, but at this point we are being reminded that the possibilities of existence are always conditioned by the facticity of existence. The existent is never pure possibility, but always factical possibility. Of course, this was implicit in the first rough sketch of existence. It was said then that existence is characterized by "mineness"; I have to be this particular existent that expresses itself as "I", and no other. This means that I have to take over whatever is already given in this particular existence—factors like race, sex, intelligence, emotional stability and all the "raw material", so to speak, out of which I have either to attain myself or fail to be myself.

Another expression which Heidegger uses in connection with these ideas is the word "thrownness". Affective states light up the "there" of *Dasein*, the actual situation in which he finds himself; but where he comes from and where he is going remain hidden, and the brute facticity of his existence stands out against this hidden background. "This characteristic of *Dasein's* Being— this "that it is"—is veiled in its "whence" and "whither", yet disclosed in itself all the more unveiledly; we call it the "thrownness" of this entity into its "there"; indeed, it is thrown in such a way that, as Being-in-the-world, it is the "there" '.[18]

These remarks show us the important role played by moods or affective states in Heidegger's existential analytic. We cannot produce a mood at will, and perhaps we commonly evade

[18] Op. cit., p. 174.

certain moods and the kinds of disclosures which they bring. But we are always in some affective state or other, and moods keep breaking in on us. "A mood assails us. It comes neither from 'outside' nor from 'inside', but arises out of Being-in-the-world, as a way of such Being.' [19]

We turn now from moods to understanding, the other fundamental way in which Being-in-the-world is disclosed to itself. Understanding too is an *existentiale*. All understanding has its moods, and likewise every mood has its own understanding, even if this is kept suppressed.

If moods have to do primarily with the disclosure of the facticity of *Dasein*, understanding has to do with the disclosure of its possibilities. Here we have to bear in mind that when we talk of "possibility" in an existential sense, we do not mean a bare contingency, something that might happen to the *Dasein* ; we mean rather a way of Being that is open to the *Dasein* in some situation or other, and into which it can move forward. Since then understanding discloses the possibilities of *Dasein*, such understanding is founded on practical concern. The fundamental kind of understanding has to do with "being able to manage something", "being a match for it", "being competent to do something",[20] and a purely theoretical understanding is derived from this broader existential kind by a process of abstraction, in which *Dasein's* practical interests are minimized.

The characteristic structure of understanding is the projection. *Dasein* is always projecting. The expression seems to get used in various ways by Heidegger : *Dasein* projects itself into its possibilities, but it also projects its possibilities upon the things that it discovers in the world. Indeed, this is how its world is built up. As *Dasein* projects its possibilities upon things and discovers them in their serviceability and usability (or, it may be, in their detrimentality), these things are incorporated into the significant world, and are understood.

The notion of projection also helps to explain more fully

[19] Op. cit., p. 176.
[20] Op. cit., p. 183.

what was meant when, in the first sketch of existence, it was said that *Dasein* is never complete in its Being but is always on its way, so that we can never, as it were, pin it down and grasp its essence. We can say that at any given moment, *Dasein* is ahead of itself, for it has already projected itself into some possibilities of its Being. Thus we can also say that at any given moment, *Dasein* is more than it actually appears on inspection, supposing that someone had come along and was trying to make an inventory of the *Dasein's* properties, as he might in the case of an object that was simply present-at-hand.

Understanding also implies interpretation. This follows from what has already been said about the way *Dasein* understandingly incorporates things into his world. Whatever he encounters gets related to the totality of understanding that he already has. But this is an act of interpretation. We have assigned the thing a place in our world and related it to the other things there, and in so doing, we have also assigned it a meaning. Meanings are not just arbitrarily stuck on to things ; they consist in relating things to the world of understanding which we already bring with us.

There are two structures or moments necessary to interpretation. One of these is the fore-structure : before we can interpret, we must bring along some kind of frame of reference, some way of seeing and conceiving phenomena. "An interpretation is never a presuppositionless apprehending of something presented to us."[21] In other words, interpretation always takes place on the basis of a prior understanding. The second structure in interpretation is the as-structure : we interpret something as something, and indeed only then can we be said to have appropriated an understanding of it. For instance, we interpret a moving light in the sky as an aircraft or as a meteorite or in some other way.

It is worth noting that Heidegger distinguishes two levels of interpretation. There is an informal, almost unconscious

[21] Op. cit., pp. 191-2.

kind of interpretation that goes on all the time. For instance, we rarely or never hear a pure noise—it is heard as already interpreted, so that we say that we hear the wind or the traffic or whatever it may be. This informal kind of interpretation would seem to be present not only in the simplest acts of understanding but even in our everyday perception of the world. But there is also formal interpretation, as, for instance, when we take up the explicit task of interpreting a poem or a play, or even of interpreting an historical event or man himself. For this kind of interpretation, men have tried to work out definite hermeneutical principles, and we have already taken note of Heidegger's interest in hermeneutics and his awareness of the "hermeneutical circle". The nature of this circle and its inevitability has been further clarified through this discussion of understanding and interpretation, for Heidegger believes that what holds for the informal type of interpretation is valid also for the more sophisticated kinds.

In *Being and Time*, his stress is on the prior understanding that we bring to interpretation, and on the need to clarify our presuppositions and, as it were, train our sights properly on what is to be interpreted. "What is decisive is not to get out of the circle but to come into it in the right way. This circle of understanding is not an orbit in which any random kind of knowledge may move ; it is the expression of the existential fore-structure of *Dasein* itself. It is not to be reduced to the level of a vicious circle, or even of a circle which is merely tolerated. In the circle is hidden a positive possibility of the most primordial kind of knowing. To be sure, we genuinely take hold of this possibility only when, in our interpretation, we have understood that our first, last and constant task is never to allow our fore-having, fore-sight and fore-conception to be presented to us by fancies and popular conceptions, but rather to make the scientific theme secure by working out these fore-structures in terms of the things themselves".[22]

[22] Op. cit., p. 195.

The discussion of interpretation leads on naturally to the question of language. Strictly speaking, we should say that it leads to the question of discourse. By "discourse" is meant the actual living communication among existents, which gets expressed in language, that is to say, in words and sentences. In making a distinction between discourse and language, and in asserting the priority of the former, Heidegger is obviously determined to regard these phenomena also in a concrete existential way. His approach differs sharply from that of the logical positivist, who tends to analyse language in abstraction from the human or existential environment in which it has its home. Heidegger's view of the matter is nearer to that of the later Wittgenstein, with his insistence that language is to be considered in terms of its use in human society. But Heidegger, at least in his earlier writings, seems to subordinate the interpretation of language to the interpretation of existence. Language gives expression to discourse, and discourse, in turn, is said to be equally primordial with states of mind and understanding as a disclosive *existentiale* of the *Dasein*. It is discourse which articulates the intelligibility of the world. Discourse expresses Being-in-the-world.

Heidegger also thinks that the logic of discourse already implies an ontology. Our logic goes back to the Greeks, and is based on an ontology of the present-at-hand. When Heidegger sometimes speaks contemptuously of "logic" we should remember that it is this particular logic that he has in mind. But he also visualizes the possibility of finding more primordial foundations for a science of logic and language, and it is in this connection that we see him making logical analysis dependent on existential analysis. "The task of liberating grammar from logic requires beforehand a positive understanding of the basic *a priori* structure of discourse in general as an *existentiale*."[23]

The function of language seems to be to light up that which is talked about, and which, in this way, is both brought to

[23] Op. cit., p. 209.

C

expression and communicated. It is the matter itself that is
illuminated in discourse. Truth, Heidegger thinks, does not
lie in the proposition or judgment (as in the traditional corre-
spondence theories of truth) but is rather the making-unhidden
of the thing itself. This is truth as the Greeks understood it,
a-lethia, "un-hiddenness". This is at any rate the most primordial
kind of truth. Heidegger can also talk of truth as "letting-be" ;
this is understood in a positive way as the act which lets something be what it really is, or which "exposes itself to what is,
as such".[24]

But Heidegger finds that *Dasein's* possibilities for genuine
discourse and for the unconcealedness into which it leads get
diverted in everyday existence. Discourse has degenerated into
idle talk. In this, there is no letting-be of the thing as it really is.
Instead, we understand it in the way that "they" have already
interpreted it. There is no genuine communication in this kind
of talk either ; instead of lighting up what is talked about, the
language rather closes it off. The language itself gets passed
along, and often it is attended by ambiguity. Instead of leading
to disclosure and unconcealment, it rather prevents them.

The various ways in which, as we have seen, the possibilities
of *Dasein* can be perverted are summed up by Heidegger in the
phenomenon which he calls the "falling" of *Dasein*. The word
which he uses means "deterioration", and to most readers it
will suggest a comparison with the theological doctrine of a
"fall" of man. But Heidegger is at pains to make it clear that he
is not making an assertion about man's spiritual condition.
He is rather pointing to ontological possibilities, though at the
same time it seems clearly his belief that for the most part, in
his everyday existing, the *Dasein* is indeed fallen or deteriorated.
This does not mean that he has ceased to exist, in the special
sense of the word, but it does seem to point to a falling away
from what is most distinctive in existence. There is on the one
hand an absorption into the world of objects, through pre-

[24] See his essay "On the Essence of Truth" in *Existence and Being*, ed.
W. Brock (H. Regnery, Chicago, 1949), p. 306.

occupation with the tasks and concerns of the instrumental world; and on the other hand there is a deprivation of freedom through the dominance of the "they", the depersonalized collective anonymous mass.

The fallenness of the *Dasein* is described by Heidegger in various ways. It is a kind of *tranquillizing*, for it takes away from *Dasein* responsibility and the anxiety that goes with it; it is also an *alienation*, for it has diverted the *Dasein* from authentic selfhood and also from authentic community; and furthermore it is a *scattering*, for the *Dasein's* possibilities are dictated by factors outside of himself and there is lacking the cohesion and unity that belong to authentic selfhood.

The time has now come when the analysis of existence that has been set forth up to this point can all be gathered up in a comprehensive concept. The analysis has disclosed a threefold structure in existence : (*a*) *Dasein* is ahead-of-itself—here belong the phenomena of possibility, projecting, understanding ; (*b*) *Dasein* is already-in-a-world—here belong the phenomena of facticity, thrownness, affective states ; (*c*) *Dasein* is close-to-its-world, so close to it that it is absorbed in it—here belong the phenomena of falling, the "they", the scattering of possibilities. This threefold structure of possibility, facticity and falling, constituting the Being of everyday Dasein, Heidegger calls "care".

And here, Heidegger claims, the existential analytic gets confirmation from the way man has interpreted himself through the ages. For have not the poets seen in care that which is essentially and distinctively human, and that which marks off man from the "carefreeness" of animal life ?

Is this then the end of our search ? Now that it has been said that existence is constituted by care, and we have seen the outlines of its threefold structure, does anything further remain to be said ? Heidegger thinks that there is. Up till now, we have been considering *Dasein* for the most part in terms of everyday routine existing, and we must now attempt to get a deeper and more primordial understanding of existence.

Toward Authentic Existence

How can the existential analytic be extended beyond the point that has been reached ? There are two ways in which this might be attempted, though we may well find that these two ways eventually converge. The first way is to try to see *Dasein* as a whole rather than in his fragmented aspects ; and the second is to inquire about the authentic *Dasein*, for so far we have had in view the everyday *Dasein* and we have seen how much of our everyday existing is moulded by patterns imposed on it from outside, and is therefore not "authentic", in the sense of being our own, something that we have definitely chosen. Heidegger seeks to break out of the limitations belonging to the earlier part of the analytic by turning attention to two further phenomena : death, the consideration of which enables us to grasp *Dasein* in its wholeness ; and conscience, which discloses to the *Dasein* its authentic possibility. Yet we shall find that these two are closely related.

But before we directly consider death and conscience, let us cast our thoughts back for a few moments to those affective states which, according to Heidegger, play an important part in the process whereby the *Dasein* becomes disclosed to itself. These states of mind, we have seen, light up the situations in which we find ourselves at any given time, for we are always already in some factical situation that delimits the possibilities open to us at that time. Fear, joy and boredom were mentioned as examples of such states of mind, and it was mentioned that Heidegger attaches special importance to the state of anxiety. We must now try to see what this special importance is.

It is claimed that anxiety is the basic state of mind, or way in which we find ourselves. But true anxiety is very rarely experienced. The falling of *Dasein*, that is to say, his tendency to let his existence be absorbed into the world or the collective mass, can also be considered as a flight from himself. So he flees also from anxiety, for this is the very mood that discloses himself in the most basic way. The main difference between anxiety and

other related states of mind (such as fear) is that anxiety seems
to have no special object, as fear has. It is not some particular
situation that gets disclosed in anxiety (though it may well be a
particular situation that arouses it on any given occasion)
but man's total situation as the existent thrown into a world
where he is and has to be. "When anxiety has subsided, then in
our everyday way of talking we are accustomed to say that 'it
was really nothing'."[25] But it may be that this everyday talk of
the "nothing" says more than we are aware of, and is already
an acknowledgement of the radical nullity and finitude of
existence, disclosed in anxiety. It is as if *Dasein*, in its very
Being, has an awareness of a standing threat to this Being.

The word "anxiety" is not perhaps a very good English
equivalent for the German word *Angst*. Other translations, such
as "dread", are even less satisfactory. The trouble about such
words is that they seem to suggest that this state of mind is a
weakness on the part of the *Dasein*—a weakness that perhaps
he could overcome, and that some people do in fact seem to
overcome. But this is a misunderstanding of Heidegger's
concept, which (as he himself acknowledges) is continuous
with Kierkegaard's idea of anxiety, though also in some regards
distinct from it. A study of both of these writers makes it clear
that one needs quite a lot of fortitude to be able to endure the
kind of anxiety of which they speak—and presumably it is for
this reason that we commonly try to avoid this mood or to
tranquillize it when it threatens to trouble us. As related to death,
anxiety asks us to face and accept the transient character of our
existence, which is through and through finite and threatened
with annulment. But anxiety is also related to conscience, and
here it asks us to face and accept responsibility for our existence
—a responsibility which, the more deeply we feel it, the more it
must destroy every trace of complacency.

Anxiety, then, discloses finitude, and the most obvious mark
of human finitude is death. It is in terms of death that Heidegger

[25] *Being and Time*, p. 231.

tries to make good the first of the two defects in the earlier analyses. Death, it is claimed, is the phenomenon that allows the *Dasein* to be grasped as a whole.

But how can this be ? Surely death is a purely negative phenomenon. It is the end and indeed the destruction of the *Dasein* as a Being-in-the-world, and in this respect it seems to be utterly unlike the various *existentialia* (affective states, understanding, discourse and the like) under which we have so far tried to reach an understanding of the structure of existence. Yet so long as it is alive, the *Dasein* is always incomplete and ahead of itself, projecting itself into its possibilities. So it might seem that while the *Dasein* is alive, it can never be grasped in its completeness ; yet when death supervenes, the *Dasein* itself has disappeared, and cannot be grasped at all.

Heidegger's long and subtle discussion of death and dying constitutes one of the most interesting chapters of *Being and Time*.[26] He freely acknowledges that death is not an end in the sense of a rounding off of existence, for death frequently strikes before a man's powers have matured, and perhaps even more often it delays until after a man's powers have declined. Death does not complete existence in the sense of bringing it to the ripeness of its potentialities. But death does set a boundary. It marks off the *Dasein*, as Being-in-the-world, from the nothing into which he disappears when he ceases to be in the world ; and to be marked off from nothing in this way is precisely to stand out from it, that is to say, to "ex-sist". Moreover, it is to exist authentically, for when one has become aware of the boundary of existence, then one has also recognized that this is one's *own* existence. Heidegger does in fact often talk of death as one's *ownmost* possibility ; and an existence that is authentic is exactly an existence that has been made one's very own.

If there is no thought of death, and the future is regarded as stretching out indefinitely, then there is no great sense of urgency or responsibility in life. In the inauthentic mode of

[26] Op. cit., pp. 279-311.

existing, *Dasein* covers up the fact of death and its concreteness. As evidence of this, Heidegger points to our everyday ways of talking about death. Frequently we use euphemisms, and the whole matter is treated impersonally. It is recognized that everyone dies, but one's own death is considered as belonging to the indefinite future.

Heidegger does not indeed encourage a meditative brooding upon death, but because death is one's ownmost possibility, the one that belongs to each person inalienably and that marks off his being, he assigns to the anticipation of death a special role in his idea of an authentic existence. All existence may be considered as a Being-toward-death, an existence in the face of the end, but to recognize this fact rather than to flee from it is to have turned toward an authentic existence. Although Heidegger does not use the expression, we might say that what he has in mind is an "eschatological "existence, that is to say, an existence that knows the urgency and responsibility of living before the imminent end, and that is shaped and unified by its awareness of the end. We have seen that one of the characteristics of a fallen or deteriorated existence is that its possibilities are scattered and incoherent.[27] But to anticipate death and to recognize the boundary of one's existence is to achieve an overarching unity that gathers up the possibilities of existence. We may think of all the possibilities of life as lying this side of the final, decisive possibility of death, so that it is in the face of death that they must be organized into a coherent pattern. Again, the expression is not Heidegger's own, but it may be helpful to us to think of death as a kind of "perspective" ; just as a picture is organized and unified by the convergence of its perspectives toward the vanishing-point, so in human life death is the unifying point around which the possibilities of life are to be organized.

Is this philosophy of Heidegger then a kind of philosophy of death ? Is it an expression of despair or nihilism ? We are not

[27] See above, p. 27

yet in a position to answer these questions. Admittedly, this looks like a somewhat grim philosophy, yet we can hardly help becoming impressed with the fact that death, from being a merely negative and destructive phenomenon, is receiving something like an affirmative character in the existential analytic. The claim is being made that it introduces a wholeness and unity into the existence of the *Dasein*.

But now we must look at Heidegger's account of conscience.[28] Just as the phenomenon of death was supposed to overcome the deficiency of the earlier analyses by allowing us to see *Dasein* in its wholeness, so, it is claimed, the phenomenon of conscience will allow us to see *Dasein* in its authenticity.

Conscience (in most languages, the word seems to have originally meant simply "consciousness") is, like affective states and understanding, one of the modes in which the *Dasein* is disclosed to itself. Conscience is precisely the disclosure to someone of what he *ought* to be, of his authentic self. One of the basic characteristics of existence, it will be remembered, is that the existent has a relation to himself. He has an idea of himself, and can either be at one with himself or estranged from himself. He can either attain or fall short.

Conscience is the awareness of how it is with oneself. It has the character of a call or a summons, and this is simply the call of the authentic self to the self in its actual absorption in the world or lostness in the "they". We need not suppose that the call comes to one from outside of himself. The call of conscience can be adequately understood in terms of the complex structure of the human existent himself. This conscience of which Heidegger speaks is to be distinguished from the everyday conscience. This is simply the voice of society, or the *superego*, in Freud's terminology. It reflects the conventions that "they" have adopted. So this everyday conscience is neither authentic itself nor conducive to an authentic existence. It is just another way in which "they" stifle and dominate the individual, and take away his own possibilities from him. This may seem to be a somewhat dangerous doctrine which encourages the rejection of conventional morality. On the other hand, moral progress only takes place when some individuals do follow insights of conscience that have broken free from the conventional standards ; and if Heidegger's doctrine seems at first sight to set the individual over against society, we have to remember his earlier statement that Being-with is a fundamental *existentiale* of the *Dasein*,[29] so that community would be an indispensable dimension of any authentic existence, and the conscience could not call to an authenticity that rejected community.

Nevertheless, because *Dasein* is in his everydayness lost in the collective inauthentic mass, the first step toward his authenticity must be to isolate him from the mass. It is here that we see the connection between conscience and death in Heidegger's thought, for it is death, as the ownmost possibility, that isolates the existent and permits him to be confronted with his true self. Conscience summons the existent to take upon himself the being that is delivered over to death and to project himself resolutely upon it. An authentic existence is in fact a resolute as opposed to an irresolute existence. The latter is scattered, but the former keeps the end in view and in doing so achieves not only a wholeness but also, according to Heidegger, a certain joy in the dispersion of illusions and the exercise of a genuinely free existence. All this may seem a strange description of authentic human existence. But before we dismiss it as nihilistic or antinomian or whatever else, we must see it in the context of Heidegger's entire philosophy.

Temporality and History

The existential analytic has now reached a point where a new synthesis becomes possible. We have already seen how the

[29] See above, p. 18

concept of care gathered up the phenomena that had been explored up to that stage in the analysis.[30] But now that something has been said about the *Dasein* in its wholeness and authenticity, can there be given a more primordial interpretation of the basic constitution of existence? Can we penetrate still further, and ask what is the fundamental structure that makes care possible?

Already in the preliminary sketch of existence, Heidegger had rejected the supposition that the existent can be conceived as a substance or understood in the categories appropriate to substances. When one talks of "substance", the model, so to speak, is the solid enduring thing, and thinghood is not a useful category for the understanding of personal existence. When existence got defined as care, it was clear that we had moved far from any notion of a substantial soul as the basis for existence, and care itself seems so elusive and volatile that we are left wondering just what does constitute human existence. In the subsequent sketch of an authentic existence, we have seen that genuine selfhood is not something ready-made (like a substantial soul that is there from the beginning) but is rather a condition that may be either gained or lost in the concrete acts and decisions of existence. Can we then find a clearer model that will help us to understand the structure of existence and selfhood and that will be more adequate to the complex and dynamic character of personal life than was the traditional model of the substantial soul?

The new model which Heidegger offers us is temporality, with its three dimensions of the present, what has been, and what is to come. These make care possible, and it is obvious that the three dimensions of temporality correspond to the threefold structure of care, as possibility (the projecting of what is to come), facticity (the taking over of what has been) and falling (the concern with the present). This notion of existence as temporality helps to sharpen the distinction between the *Dasein*

[30] See above, p. 27.

and the thing or even the animal. The thing (substance) endures
through time. It is in time, and changes with time. But its
relation to time is that of moving from one "now" to another,
so that at any given moment, its past is "no longer" and its
future is "not yet". Its relation to time is thus an external one.
The existent, on the other hand, is not simply confined to the
"now". As projecting, he is already in the future, while as
thrown, he is always one who has already been. He is not
simply "in time", moving along from one now to the next;
rather, he takes time and has time. Of course, in the inauthentic
mode of existence, the *Dasein*, as he gets scattered in immediate
concerns, tends to be like those entities which simply "hop"
from moment to moment. But this is a fallen or deteriorated
existence. In any case, we may suppose that the *Dasein* never
quite becomes just another object, enduring through time.
But clearly it is in an authentic existence that the dimensions of
temporality are most fully unified and that true selfhood is
attained. The existent who has projected himself on death has
already penetrated to the boundary of what is to come ; while
in responding to conscience by taking over in responsibility
his factical guiltiness, he has appropriated that which has been.
It is through this appropriation of both the "ahead" and the
"already" that he is freed for authentic resoluteness in the
present situation. The authentic *Dasein* displays "the unity of a
future which makes present in the process of having been ;
we designate it as 'temporality'." [31]

The central place which Heidegger gives to temporality in
his analysis implies that his philosophy is a secular one, in the
strict meaning of the word "secular". Yet although the existent is
constituted by temporality and although his life is one of care,
terminated by death, he is not simply "in time". In so far as he
transcends the "now" and attains to genuine selfhood, he is
realizing a kind of "eternal life" in the midst of time.

To recognize the fundamentally temporal character of

---

[31] *Being and Time*, p. 374.

existence is also to recognize that it is historical. Our attention
has been mostly directed to the individual existent, and perhaps
in Heidegger as in other philosophers of existence there is a
tendency toward individualism, though this is mainly in reaction
against that false collectivism which stifles the possibilities of
the individual *Dasein*. But it will be remembered that the
existential analytic found that Being-with belongs intrinsically
to the constitution of existence, and that *Dasein's* world is a
common world. Hence the temporality of every individual
existence is caught up in the wider movement of history, and
every individual shares in the destiny of his generation or of his
age. Furthermore, there is disclosed to the individual not only
the past, present and future of his own existence, but likewise
the past, present and future of the historical community to
which he belongs.

History has been understood in many ways. The very word
is ambiguous, for we use it both for the historical actuality,
the stream of history, as we sometimes call it, and also for the
study of history. Heidegger avoids this confusion by using
two distinct words in German : *Geschichte* for the actual historical
process, and *Historie* for the study of this process. But the two
are closely connected, because it is only on account of the fact
that he is himself through and through historical that the human
existent can undertake the study of history. In making this
statement, Heidegger acknowledges that he is following the
teaching of Wilhelm Dilthey, who made a sharp distinction
between the natural and the human sciences. The human
sciences are possible only because we directly participate in
their subject-matter. We can only study history because, as
historical existents ourselves, we have first-hand acquaintance
with the historical reality. We know what it is to deliberate, to
decide, to aspire, to cherish ambitions and so on. A historian
who only reported facts or connections and concatenations of
facts would not be penetrating to the reality of history. One
could spend a lot of time and ingenuity in discovering how
many times Plato visited Sicily, but the knowledge of such

facts alone does not even begin to open up the historical reality of Plato.[32]

Heidegger is concerned to make two main points about history. The first is that we are mistaken in thinking that history has to do with the past. Human existence is always historical, and indeed history is oriented to the future. In studying history, we are studying man, and we are studying man in order to learn about the possibilities of his existence. The hermeneutic circle comes into view once more in this discussion of history. It is because we are ourselves historical in our being that we can take up the study of history ; yet in so far as this study discloses to us what the possibilities of human existence are, we reach through it an enlarged self-understanding. Perhaps one could cite a man like Sir Winston Churchill as illustrating the kind of thing that Heidegger has in mind. Churchill was a keen student of history, and his own experience of affairs made him a discriminating judge of the historical material. Yet his historical studies were in turn brought to bear on the contemporary political problems with which he had to deal, and what they disclosed of human existence contributed to the decisions which he made. Heidegger's second point follows from the first. If history has to do primarily not with past facts but with human existence whether past, present or future, then history must be studied existentially. It is true that the historian has to concern himself with documents, monuments and many other things that have come down from the past, and that in dealing with these, he must use, as far as possible, the methods of empirical science. But these things are only secondarily historical, that is to say, they are historical only through their association with human persons. The human existent himself is the primary historical, and the human existent is to be understood existentially rather than in the categories appropriate to empirically observable objects.

So Heidegger seems to be saying that the stuff of history, so

[32] Cf. *Being and Time*, p. 452.

to speak, is possibility rather than fact. But does this not abolish the distinction between history and fiction or mythology? Heidegger does not think so. Indeed, he believes that history is just as strict a study as mathematics, though it differs in having broader existential foundations.[33] What we see in history are the *factical* possibilities of existence, and these are not to be confused with merely utopian or imaginary possibilities.

Presumably the historian is not interested in all the factical possibilities that are exhibited in the story of mankind. He selects those that stand out from the routine and the everyday and that disclose new and unsuspected dimensions of the *Dasein*. History is concerned above all with the exploration of the authentic possibilities of existence. Here we must notice another idea which Heidegger introduces in the course of his discussion of history—the idea of "repetition". History reveals the authentic repeatable possibilities of *Dasein*. The word "repeatable" is perhaps rather too weak to translate the German *wiederholbar*. Father Richardson gets the active sense of the word better by translating it "retrievable".[34] Repetition is not just a mechanical reproducing, but rather a going into the past in such a way that one fetches back the possibility which it contains and makes-present this possibility in our existence now. There is even a kind of violence in such interpretation of history. The past has to be seized and broken open, as it were. It becomes significant for the future, and might almost be said to get integrated with the future in the moment of vision and decision. Certainly Heidegger has in mind a much more lively and intrinsic relation to history than just that of searching in the past for some parallels that might be imitated today. "The theme of historical study is neither that which has happened just once for all nor something universal that floats above it, but the possibility which has been factically existent. This possibility does not get repeated as such—that is to say, understood in an authentically

---

[33] Op. cit., p. 195.
[34] *Heidegger: through Phenomenology to Thought* (Nijhoff, The Hague: 1963). p. 89.

historical way—if it becomes perverted into the colourlessness of a supratemporal model. Only by historicality which is factical and authentic can the history of what has-been-there, as a resolute fate, be disclosed in such a manner that in repetition the 'force' of the possible gets struck home into one's factical existence—in other words, that it comes toward that existence in its futural character." [35]

Heidegger's understanding of history may best be illustrated from his own treatment of the history of Western philosophy. As is well-known, the pre-Socratic thinkers, especially Heraclitus and Parmenides, have exercised a great fascination on his mind. But his interest in them is not merely antiquarian. It is an attempt to repeat or retrieve the seminal insights of Western thought in such a way as would renew the philosophy of our own time. In the words of a scholar who has devoted special attention to Heidegger's relations to the pre-Socratics, "we return to the origins of this our Western tradition of philosophy in order to rebuild anew, to build in an authentically historical manner upon the basis of these origins. In other words, Heidegger's restudy of the pre-Socratic origins of Western thinking is meant to be historical in the full Heideggerian sense of that word, namely, creative for the future possibilities of *Dasein*". [36]

Heraclitus and Parmenides are often contrasted, but Heidegger sees them as at one in raising the question of Being in a fundamental way. But almost immediately the question began to be side-tracked, and interest moved from Being to the beings. This began to happen with Plato and Aristotle, and the subsequent history of Western philosophy has been one of the forgetting of Being. Thus Heidegger does not think of the history of philosophy as a history of progress. It is, he declares, a "basic fallacy" to believe "that history begins with the primitive and backward, the weak and helpless. The opposite is true. The beginning is the strongest and mightiest. What comes

[35] *Being and Time*, p. 447.
[36] George Joseph Seidel, O.S.B., *Martin Heidegger and the Pre-Socratics* (Lincoln : University of Nebraska Press, 1964), p. 29.

afterwards is not development but the flattening that results from mere spreading out; it is inability to maintain the beginning; the beginning is emasculated and exaggerated into a caricature of greatness taken as purely numerical and quantitative size and extension." [37]

It was Heidegger's intention at one time to write a part of *Being and Time* that would bear the title : *Destruktion der Ontologie*. This should not be understood so much as a "destruction" as a kind of "dismantling", a going back through the history of philosophy to find where the forgetting of Being has taken place so that, once again, the genuine insights may be recovered and made creative in our own time. Although the formal *Destruktion der Ontologie* was not written, Heidegger's many writings on the outstanding philosophers of the Western tradition show us clearly how the dismantling and reconstruction proceed. His interpretations of these philosophers are often highly unconventional, and show that violence or breaking open which he considers an essential part of the hermeneutic art. The true interpreter has to hear not only what was said but what was left unsaid. Some critics think that Heidegger's interpretations are purely arbitrary and guided by his own presuppositions, but there is no doubt that in many ways he does gain remarkable insights from his attempts at repetitive thinking. Certainly his *Destruktion* is by no means a purely negative approach to the philosophical tradition.

A good example is afforded by his treatment of Kant. His book on Kant[38] was first written in 1929, and reflects the historical teaching of *Being and Time*, as well as pointing forward to Heidegger's later thought. Probably the most interesting part of the discussion concerns Kant's obscure doctrine of the schematism of the categories, that "hidden art in the depth of the soul" whereby the bare intellectual categories become

---

[37] *An Introduction to Metaphysics*, tr. Ralph Manheim (Yale University Press ; New Haven: 1959), p. 155.
[38] *Kant and the Problem of Metaphysics*, tr. James Churchill (Indiana University Press, Bloomington : 1962).

capable of application to actual sensuous phenomena. As is well-known, Kant's argument turns on the notion of time, and, according to one of his commentators, "it suggests the possibility of making a fresh start, and of justifying the categories from the nature of time without any reference to the forms of judgment".[39] In any case, Heidegger interprets the doctrine as meaning that Kant was moving toward the thought of man as the existent who is constituted by temporality, rather than of man as traditionally conceived in terms of his rational and logical nature. But Kant did not carry through his insight, and in fact retreated from it (or so Heidegger thinks) in the second edition of the *Critique of Pure Reason*.

Kant's retreat—or alleged retreat—is typical of the Western philosophical tradition. It has become dominated more and more by the logic of the present-at-hand and has more and more forgotten Being. Nietzsche represents the culmination of this tendency in the West, for with him, Being is dismissed as a mere empty word and the subjective will to power and domination finds expression. This philosophy ushers in the age of technology, and it is in this age that Heidegger seeks to recall men to a deeper level of existence and to rekindle the question of Being.

The Meaning of Being

Our account of the fate of Being in the history of Western thought brings us back to the question from which this exposition of Heidegger's thought set out—the question of the meaning of Being. We have already noted how Heidegger's thinking has fallen into two major phases. The earlier phase was dominated by the inquiry into human existence, though this inquiry was undertaken not for its own sake, but as the most promising way into the question of Being. The later phase is concerned directly with Being, and man himself is

[39] H. J. Paton, *Kant's Metaphysic of Experience* (Allen & Unwin, London: 1936), vol. II, p. 20.

D

now understood in the light of Being. It is this later phase
which must now engage our attention.

Already in the inaugural lecture which Heidegger gave when
he took up his duties at Freiburg in 1929, we find both some of
the characteristics of his later thought and the links that connect
this with his earlier existential investigations. This lecture
dealt with the question, "What is metaphysics ? " [40] and did
so concretely by taking up a particular metaphysical question,
for Heidegger held that every metaphysical question involves
the whole of metaphysics. But the particular question which he
took up seems a strange one indeed, for it is the question of—
nothing !

Heidegger's lecture was given before the academic community,
made up of the professors of the various sciences and particular
disciplines, and it might well seem nowadays that when the
specialized scholars in the various fields have done their work,
then there is indeed nothing left for the philosopher. But
perhaps only a very bold philosopher would blandly announce
that he proposed to take for the theme of his lecture precisely
this nothing.

Heidegger began his lecture with a mention of the wide
variety of subjects studied in a university. The total field of
knowledge today is broken up among many disciplines, yet
they all have one characteristic in common—they claim to deal
with what is, with the beings, with the things that really are.
Man, who is himself a being, irrupts into the world of beings
and tries to understand them both for what they are and how
they are. Modern science claims to be docile before the real.
It is objective and factual. It treats of what is, and nothing else.

This is the cue for Heidegger's discussion of nothing. How
about this "nothing else" ? The sciences are not interested in
it, though indeed they speak of it when, to emphasize their

[40] *Was ist Metaphysik?* (Vittorio Klostermann, Frankfurt-am-Main:
7th edition, with introduction and postscript, 1949). There is an English
translation of the lecture and postscript in *Existence and Being*, ed. W. Brock
(Henry Regnery, Chicago: 1949).

objectivity, they claim to be dealing with what is *and nothing else*. The question about this "nothing else", left aside by the sciences, is a metaphysical question.

The beginning of Heidegger's lecture is so paradoxical that we may feel we are being somehow mesmerized. Is there not a verbal trick here, when a casual reference to "nothing else" gets exalted into a metaphysical theme ? Or again, is there not an elementary error in logic, whereby the pronoun "nothing" is getting understood as if it denoted "something" ? These critical questions, I think, must be laid aside for the present until we see how Heidegger develops the theme of his lecture.

Heidegger's argument is that the idea of "nothing" is not, as is commonly supposed, derived from a more general idea of "negation". Rather, it is the other way round. The general idea of negation is derived from the concrete encounter with "nothing" that the *Dasein* has in its very being. It is here that the definite link between the ontological and the existential aspects of Heidegger's philosophy is established. We remember the importance which Heidegger attached to the disclosive mood of anxiety, and how this mood lights up for us the character of human existence as delivered over to death.[41] It is this concrete encounter with the nothingness that essentially belongs to a Being-toward-death that is claimed by Heidegger as the fundamental meaning of "nothing" and the existential basis for the logical idea of negation.

But the notion of anxiety is developed further. In a genuine mood of anxiety, not only is one aware of the finitude of human existence : it is claimed that the totality of beings sinks into nothing. "All things, and we with them, sink into a kind of indifference . . . The only thing that remains and overwhelms us while the beings slip away is this 'nothing'. Anxiety reveals nothing."[42]

Is this something like an encounter with nothing, a pre-logical nothing rooted in the very way we are and making

[41] See above, pp. 28-9
[42] *Was ist Metaphysik?*, p. 32.

possible logical negation ? Furthermore, when one talks of an "encounter with nothing", this does not mean just that there has been no encounter at all. The nothing that is encountered is certainly not a "something" or an object. In Heidegger's way of expressing the matter, the nothing is not even apprehended, but it is manifest. It is manifest not as alongside the beings or additional to them, but in and through them, as if in a sense it were a constituent of them. Obviously, if we think of the matter for a moment, all finite and determinate beings are what they are only to the extent that we can recognize what they are not. Pure undifferentiated Being would actually be indistinguishable from sheer nothing. It is the nihilation of the nothing that is said to bring *Dasein* face to face with the beings *as* beings. In other words, it is only against the background of nothing that anything stands out as something that is. Against this foil of nothing, we notice the wonder that *there is something*. Heidegger reformulates the ancient dictum *ex nihilo nihil fit* as : *ex nihilo omne ens qua ens fit*.[43] His lecture ends with the question : "Why beings at all, rather than just nothing ?"

The questions and objections that spring to mind as Heidegger unfolds his lecture on nothing are dealt with in the later post-script. Specifically, he faces three objections, and his discussion of these goes far toward clarifying the lecture itself and toward showing how it anticipates the later developments of his philosophy.

The first objection is that the lecture presents us with an unmitigated nihilism. It makes nothing the theme of meta-physics and seems to exalt it to a key position. It even seems to be suggested that everything becomes a matter of indifference, so that it hardly matters whether one lives or dies. But Heidegger strongly contests such an interpretation. The true nihilism, he claims, is the forgetting of Being that aims only at the mastery of beings. For the "nothing" of which Heidegger talks, the "nothing else" which is of no interest to the sciences, turns

[3] Op. cit., p. 40.

out to be nothing less than Being. We have been clear from the beginning[44] that Being cannot be considered as itself a being, something which is ; therefore, from the point of view that is interested only in what is, and nothing else, Being belongs to the nothing else. Just as death in Heidegger's existential analysis took on a positive role as the factor which integrates existence, so in his metaphysic "nothing" is not sheerly negative but likewise plays a positive role. It is the non-entity which nevertheless has more being than any entity, for it is the Being that comes before every entity and in virtue of which any entity *is*. Being is "wholly other" to the beings, it is the *transcendens* that cannot fall under the categories applicable to beings. Yet it is so far from being nugatory that it is the most beingful of all.

A second objection alleges that by giving an important place in the analysis to the mood of anxiety and the expectation of death, the whole argument has a morbid subjective character. It may appeal to the neurotic, but hardly to the healthy-minded. This kind of objection is one that already came to our notice when we considered at an earlier stage the claim that anxiety is the basic affective state.[45] We saw then that one would need to be strong-minded rather than timorous to endure a genuine ontological anxiety. But in the context of the present argument, Heidegger develops the notion of anxiety further by relating it to the sense of awe aroused when man becomes aware of the mystery of Being—"that wonder of all wonders, that the beings *are*." [46]

Finally, there is the objection that logic has been abandoned, and there has been put in its place a philosophy of feeling. To those who find this objection cogent, then perhaps the whole of Heidegger's philosophy will seem problematical and an offence against the canons of logic and ordinary commonsense. Yet if we accept that a philosophy of Being must be built on the basis of our total confrontation with Being or our total partici-

[44] See above, p. 4
[45] See above, p. 29
[46] Op. cit., pp. 46-7.

pation in Being, throughout the range of our existing, then it may not seem so strange that this kind of philosophizing will burst out of the logic that applies in our thinking about objects within the world. We might even come to accept Heidegger's claim that the logical idea of negation itself is made possible only through a more immediate and preconceptual awareness of the "nothing". But in any case, Heidegger is not abandoning logic. Although the logic of scientific inquiry is not appropriate to ontological inquiry, this inquiry has its own logic, and Heidegger does in fact offer a description of the thinking that is peculiar to it. The notion that there is a plurality of logics and that all languages do not conform to the same criteria is nowadays a commonplace.

How then does Heidegger describe the thinking that is appropriate to the understanding of Being? We get a clue first of all from the distinction which he makes between this thinking (which he will call "primordial" or "essential" thinking) and the "calculative" thinking that is characteristic of the sciences and of our everyday activities in the world. Calculative thinking objectifies and breaks up the whole. It is directed toward the handling and mastery of the things within the world. It is, of course, a thinking that is concerned with beings, not with Being. Sometimes Heidegger will hardly allow that it is thinking at all. This is the thinking that is typical of the techno-logical age, and presumably it is the kind of thinking that may be increasingly done for us by machines, just as machines have already relieved us of the drudgeries of heavy manual labour.

We have already made acquaintance with "repetitive" thinking, the kind that enters into some authentic historical possibility and makes-present its disclosure for our own time.[47] This repetitive thinking might be a thinking of Being, and indeed it is precisely such a thinking of Being that Heidegger sought in the pre-Socratics. In such cases, Being is mediated through the historical possibility that gets repeated. But

[47] See above, p. 38.

"primordial" or "essential" thinking seems to be more direct than even repetitive thinking. It has the same passive, meditative character—it is a thinking that listens, as distinct from the busy-ness of calculative thinking. But in this primordial thinking, it would seem that the historical intermediary is no longer required. Primordial thinking is said to be an occurrence of Being in the person who thinks. In such thinking, Being has the initiative. Fragmentariness is overcome, and the truth or unveiledness of Being is preserved. Heidegger sees a parallel to this primordial thinking in the composing of the poet and in the thanking of the religious devotee. His deep appreciation of poetry, especially that of Hölderlin, is well-known. The poet is receptive in his interpretation of the world. He lets it impinge upon him, and stands in an openness to it.

Are we then to think that Heidegger abandons philosophy in order to join the poets and the mystics? Certainly, he sees a parallel between the philosophical quest for Being and the work of poets and mystics, but he does not simply identify them. Presumably the difference between the primordial thinking of the philosopher and the composing of the poet is that the former still seeks conceptual structures, while the latter employs evocative images. Both, however, are concerned with language. Perhaps this last point serves in turn to differentiate the philosopher of Being from the mystic. Heidegger does indeed use a quasi-mystical and religious language. The passive, receptive thinking which he advocates for the philosopher is called by him "abandonment" or "releasement",[48] a word that was used by Meister John Eckhart and that has a long history in Christian spirituality. But whereas the mystic may claim a direct vision of God, Heidegger thinks of the encounter with Being as one that is mediated through language. Heidegger is very insistent that language is not something that man invents. It is as much a part of environing Being as is nature and its phenomena. "The difference is only that the latter, the power that is man's environ-

[48] See especially his *Discourse on Thinking*, tr. John M. Anderson and E. Hans Freund (New York: Harper & Row, 1966).

ment, sustains, drives, inflames him, while the former reigns within him as the power which he, as the being which he himself is, must take upon himself." [49] In his essay on humanism,[50] Heidegger sharply differentiates his position from that of French existentialists such as Sartre who think of man as the measure of all things. Man is rather understood as the particular being to whom Being communicates itself, and language is understood as the "house of Being." In some of Heidegger's late essays, he seems to come near to identifying language and Being. At least, he now says about language what he formerly said about Being. It is language itself that speaks.[51] "The essence of language is the language of essence."

Much of this teaching seems like a reversal of the doctrines of *Being and Time*, and, of course, we do indeed here meet with the so-called "later" Heidegger in all his elusiveness and para-doxicality. The human *Dasein* which began by asking questions about Being now stands before Being and receives answers—or perhaps just waits for answers. Truth is now understood as the letting-be of what is, rather than as the active dis-covering of what is by the *Dasein*. Nature is an emerging presence revealing or opening itself to man. Heidegger indeed claims that the Greek word for nature, *physis*, originally meant "emerging", and he tries to connect it also with *phainomenon*, "appearance". How well-founded or ill-founded such etymological specula-tions may be is a question that can be left to the classical philologist to decide. But this style of argument in Heidegger illustrates what he means by calling language the "house of Being".

It is clear too that these ways of talking about Being, truth, language, nature, open up dimensions of the world that were left concealed when, in *Being and Time*, the world was described as an instrumental system, articulated by the significance pro-jected upon it by *Dasein's* practical concerns. But this does not

[49] *An Introduction to Metaphysics*, p. 156.
[50] *Brief über den Humanismus* (V. Klostermann, Frankfurt-am-Main: 1947).
[51] *Unterwegs zur Sprache* (Neske, Pfullingen : 1959), p. 12.

mean that the analysis presented in *Being and Time* has now been abandoned. We have to remember that the earlier analysis was specifically directed to our everyday being-in-the-world, which is said to be for the most part inauthentic. More precisely, this everyday being-in-the-world is characterized by its preoccupation with the beings and its forgetting of Being. It would seem, however, that authentic being-in-the-world is a rare phenomenon, and is attained only by a few exceptional individuals, though perhaps others have glimpses of it in situations where anxiety or conscience is allowed to speak without concealment. But it is to the artist, the poet, the philosopher, perhaps also the mystic and the prophet that Being reveals itself ; and these are men who have been isolated from the mass. There is an aristocratic element in Heidegger's philosophy. Though in many ways he expresses the mind of the twentieth century, he is also the implacable critic of the vulgarity and shallowness of mass-produced culture.

Even metaphysics gets left behind (or rather, "overcome") in Heidegger's final thought. Descartes once described philosophy as like a tree, of which the branches are the several sciences and the root is metaphysics. But traditional metaphysics too was scientific and objectifying in its thought. It was still concerned with the beings rather than with Being. Alluding to Descartes' metaphor of the tree, Heidegger indicates that we must get beyond even the root of the tree to the ground which supports the root. This ground was left out of account by traditional metaphysics, but the ground is nothing other than the light or truth of Being.[52]

What then are we finally to say about the meaning of Being, the question which has guided Heidegger's philosophy from its beginning ? Just because Being is itself the ground of intelligibility, the light in which the beings are seen, it must itself be beyond any attempt to grasp it. It eludes all the categories of thought. Hence much that Heidegger says about Being is

[52] Cf. *Der Rückgang in den Grund der Metaphysik*, prefaced to the fifth edition of *Was ist Metaphysik?*, 1949.

E

reminiscent of negative theology, as it tries to talk of the mystery of God. Being, as we have already learned, is the absolute *transcendens* and the wholly other.[53] But just as no theology is content to remain purely negative, so Heidegger's account of Being introduces more affirmative notions, albeit in an elusive and evocative fashion. Some of these notions come from etymological considerations concerning the various Indo-European roots that express "being". Thus ideas like "dwelling", "emerging", "presence" give hints of the meaning of Being. Other notions are derived from such traditional contrasts as those between Being and becoming, or between Being and appearance. As Heidegger thinks of it, Being is indeed distinct from becoming, but includes becoming, and thus is not a static, eternal Being, but has to be thought of in terms of the temporal horizon ; likewise, Being is distinct from appearance, yet is nothing apart from what appears, and so is not some "thing-in-itself" lurking behind the phenomena. And perhaps this is as far as one can go in the elucidation of the meaning of Being.

And what of man, the particular being from whom the inquiry set out ? If it appeared at first that man was to be made the measure of all things, this trend is reversed by the dialectic which finally subjects man to Being. Man remains unique as the existent, the place of openness among all the beings. But the notion of autonomous man yields to the notion of man as the responsible steward, and perhaps this is by far the more mature notion, and one that has great relevance as technological man increasingly subjects the world to his control and has its resources more and more at his disposal. Is he the absolute master, or is he rather the one to whom Being has graciously entrusted itself and on whom it has conferred an almost frightening responsibility ? Heidegger's answer is clearly given : "Man is not the lord of beings. Man is the shepherd of Being".[54]

---

[53] See above, p. 45
[54] *Brief über den Humanismus*, p. 29.

3

Significance

Now that we have before us an exposition of the main themes of Heidegger's philosophy, we must ask about his significance and try to justify what was simply asserted right at the beginning of this book: that, "by any standard, Martin Heidegger must be reckoned among the greatest and most creative philosophers of the twentieth century".[55]

Perhaps the first thing to say about Heidegger's significance is that he shows us the possibility of a philosophy which is thoroughly contemporary and yet which does not shirk the traditional philosophical problems. Heidegger is post-Kantian and post-Nietzschean, not just chronologically but in his thinking. He has "overcome" the old-style metaphysics, but he has not fallen into the error of positivism, as if that were the only way left for Western philosophy. It is true that he renounces eternity and orients his philosophy to time and history. He abolishes any supposed invisible world behind the world of phenomena. He replaces God with Being. He substitutes for stable substances and essences the fluid categories of existence. Yet in all this he finds a wholeness and meaning, a kind of intrinsic transcendence, that rescues the world from the absurdity or triviality that characterizes a mere coming-into-being and passing-out-of-being.

But how does he do this? He does it by attempting to shift the starting-point of philosophy. The philosophy of the object ends up in positivism, yet the alternative to this is not sheer subjectivism. The philosophy of existence attempts to overcome

[55] See above, p. 1

the subject-object split. It begins from concrete participation in the world, not from either observation of the phenomena "outside" of us or from introspective investigation of our own minds. We know that Heidegger is not an existentialist in the narrow sense, for his interest has always been directed to Being. Yet this should not blind us to the extraordinary contribution that he has made to existentialism. Philosophers who have little use for Heidegger's ontology acknowledge the value of his existential analytic. For instance, Marjorie Grene has written : "If we leave out of consideration the religious problems raised by Kierkegaard, the philosophical contribution of existentialism was most purely and intensely formulated in Heidegger's *Being and Time*. As the author of *Being and Time*, therefore, Heidegger occupies a unique place in the intellectual history of our time." [56]

We have seen, of course, that Heidegger moves from his existentialist starting-point into ontological reflections that may seem far removed from it. Many philosophers are doubtful about the significance of Heidegger's later work, though our own view has been that the earlier and later work constitute a unity and reflect a dialectic that is intrinsic to the question of Being.

The discussion of the significance of his work, both early and late, may be conveniently organized around four topics : (1) the doctrine of man ; (2) the problems of language and hermeneutics ; (3) thinking ; (4) the notion of Being.

(1) We begin with the doctrine of man, especially as set forth in *Being and Time*. Heidegger radically departs from such traditional notions as the substantial soul and the essentialist understanding of human nature. Existence takes precedence over essence, and man is to be understood in temporal and historical terms. Yet Heidegger equally eschews a purely empirical approach to the question of man. The metaphysical self or soul of the philosophical tradition is set aside, but the self is not

[56] *Martin Heidegger*, in the series "Studies in Modern European Literature and Thought" (Bowes & Bowes, London, 1957), pp. 11-12.

dissolved into a succession of experiences, as happened in the philosophy of Hume. Heidegger's remarkable achievement is to have provided an account of man that bursts out of the old metaphysical categories, and yet that still does justice to the spiritual (existential) constitution of man as a person.

This understanding of man is neither metaphysical nor naturalistic, and it demands to be considered alongside Freudianism, Marxism and whatever other understandings of man compete for recognition today. It may be that Heidegger's existential interpretation of man is the one that will best safeguard what is distinctively human and protect this against the threat of dehumanization.

Of all the views of man that have been current in the West perhaps it is the Christian doctrine of man that stands nearest to Heidegger's. It is surely no accident that Heidegger finds common ground in his analysis of existence with such Christian thinkers as St. Augustine, Luther and Kierkegaard. The Heideggerian categories, or, rather, *existentialia*, such as "possibility", "facticity", "falling", "being-toward-death" and others express in a modern idiom insights into man that can be found in the Bible, though there they get expressed in the antiquated terminology of an earlier time. For confirmation of this, one may compare Heidegger's existential analytic with St. Paul's way of understanding man, as this has been set forth by Bultmann.[57]

Needless to say, there are very considerable differences too between Heidegger's account of man and the Christian doctrine, and one must be aware of making oversimplified identifications, for instance, between Heidegger's concept of falling and the biblical idea of a fall of man.[58] Especially in *Being and Time*, man seems to be represented as having an autonomy that would be hard to reconcile with such biblical doctrines as those of

[57] Cf. *Theology of the New Testament*, tr. Kendrick Grobel SCM Press, London : 1952), vol. I, especially pp. 190-269.
[58] Cf. the present writer's *An Existentialist Theology* (SCM Press, London: 1955), pp. 100-111.

creation and redemption, and which Sartre and others can be excused for having interpreted as a thoroughgoing humanism, with man as the creator of all meaning and value. But the later writings bring the explicit rejection of such a humanism, and we have seen that man's position is represented as that of a steward rather than that of a master, and clearly this is much closer to the Christian understanding.

(2) We turn now to our second topic, Heidegger's treatment of the problem of language and hermeneutics. Here again, one has to take account of the different emphases found in the earlier and later writings.

In *Being and Time*, what seems to be important in the treatment of language (or discourse) [59] is the insistence that it be understood as a human phenomenon or an *existentiale*. Naturalistic accounts of language have concentrated attention on the question of how language refers to things and events in the world. Certainly this is one dimension of language, but there are other dimensions as well, and it is to these that *Being and Time* directs our view. In language, man expresses himself, that is to say, his own being-in-the-world; and likewise he communicates with the other. Expressing and communicating are just as essential to language as is referring, but expressing and communicating have a distinctly human and existential character. Heidegger correlates language analysis with existential analysis, and this is certainly a more concrete way of taking language than one finds in abstract logical analysis. The later Wittgenstein seems to have moved in the direction of Heidegger's concreteness when he insisted on setting language in its living context and when indeed he went so far as to call language "a form of life". [60]

In any case, to understand language as the expression of existence is to allow for possibilities of interpretation which are ruled out where empirical referring is taken to be the

---

[59] See above, p. 25
[60] *Philosophical Investigations*, tr. G. E. M. Anscombe (Blackwell, Oxford : 1953), p. 19e.

standard function of language. It makes possible the existential interpretation of such language forms as myth, which appears to be fantastic if we take its statements as objective empirical propositions, but which can make very good sense when these same statements are interpreted as expressions of man's self-understanding. The best-known example of such existential interpretation is Bultmann's demythologizing of the New Testament, in the course of which he is able to infuse new life and meaning into such notions as eschatology, by translating these out of the archaic objectifying language of myth into an existential language of self-understanding. Another good illustration of this kind of existential interpretation is provided by Hans Jonas' brilliant work in the field of Gnosticism. But it might be worthwhile posing the question whether Bultmann's use of Heidegger's philosophy as an interpretative tool could have been successful unless there had been, as we have suggested, an affinity between Heidegger's understanding of human existence and the biblical doctrine of man ; and likewise whether Jonas' use of the Heideggerian concepts was not made possible by the even closer affinity between existentialism and Gnosticism.[61]

Heidegger's later thoughts on language and hermeneutics shift attention away from the existential characteristics of language. Instead of insisting that man expresses himself in language, we are told that language itself speaks, or that language is the voice of Being. Interpretation demands that we be open to the address of Being, rather than that we attempt an existential translation of what is said. It follows that the hermeneutic rules which one might lay down for demythologizing are inadequate to this listening, passive kind of interpretation, which could hardly be formulated in rules at all. Such interpretation is not so much a science as an art, or perhaps even a *charisma*. The significance of this shift in Heidegger's thought is that it makes room for the notion of interpretation that one finds in Karl Barth. There are some remarkable parallels between Heidegger's

---

[61] Jonas himself has an interesting discussion of the point. See *The Gnostic Religion* (Beacon Press, Boston : 2nd edition, 1963), pp. 320-1.

teaching on language as the voice of Being and Barth's conception of the Word of God.

But in so far as both styles of interpretation are embraced within Heidegger's dialectic, he may be said to point to a more adequate solution to the hermeneutical problem than either Bultmann or Barth, taken separately. Heidegger's solution lies beyond both of these theologians, and synthesizes their respective insights.

(3) The remarks on language and interpretation lead straight into our third topic, Heidegger's account of thinking. Heinrich Ott has indeed made use of Heidegger's concept of thinking for precisely the purpose of bridging the gulf between Barth and Bultmann.[62]

Let us remind ourselves of the main point in Heidegger's view of thinking. Although he distinguishes several kinds of thinking, the primary contrast is between calculative thinking and primordial thinking. Calculative thinking has to do with understanding, predicting and controlling empirical events, and it has an active character. Primordial thinking reflects on Being rather than on the beings, and has a receptive, passive character.

To some critics, it has seemed that Heidegger's exaltation of primordial thinking and his corresponding depreciation of calculative thinking amount to a rejection of science and technology, and even to an irresponsible withdrawal from the factical conditions of the twentieth century. To some extent, this criticism may be justified. Yet Heidegger may claim his justification too. His role is almost a prophetic one. The technological era has so many uncritical admirers and has awakened so many hopes that may never be realized that we need the critic who will point out its limitations and its ambiguities and how, if it promises enrichment of human life in some dimensions, it threatens diminution in others. The extraordinary thing about Heidegger is that he accomplishes this critique not

---

[62] Cf. *Denken und Sein* (Evangelischer Verlag, Zollikon : 1959).

by a romantic recall to a former time or by an attempt to re-
furbish ancient categories, but by opening up the forgotten
dimension of transcendence *within* the framework of contemporary thought itself.

The way that leads from existential self-understanding through
repetitive (historical) thinking to primordial thinking provides
a contemporary way of understanding and expounding the
experiences that men of religion have known as mysticism,
contemplation, revelation. And surely Heidegger is right in
claiming that without the dimension which these words name,
human life ceases to be authentic—which means that it ceases to
be fully human.

(4) The last topic to be discussed is Heidegger's notion of
Being. We have seen that there are obscurities in this notion,
and yet that we can say some things about Being. Being is the
incomparable that is wholly other to every particular being and
comes before them. Being is the *transcendens* that is nevertheless
nothing apart from the beings in which it is manifest. Being is
not static but includes becoming and perhaps even has a history.
Being takes the initiative in addressing man, in giving him
speech, in setting him in the light and openness. Being is gracious
toward man and constitutes him its guardian.

As these descriptions of Being build up, we can hardly deny
that for Heidegger, Being has something of a holy, divine
character. Certainly, Heidegger does not identify Being with
God, and yet I think it would be true to say that in his thought,
Being has taken the place of God ; for Being undoubtedly is
furnished with most of the attributes that have been traditionally
assigned to God, and Being seems to perform most of the
functions that have belonged to God. Being is the incompre-
hensible and wholly other that cannot be counted as an *ens
creatum* and yet has more reality ; Being both transcends the
world and is immanent in it ; Being is the author of revelation
and grace.

It has been sometimes suggested that Heidegger's doctrine of
Being cuts behind the old controversy between theists and

atheists, and renders it obsolete. Up to a point, this observation is correct. If the theist is taken to mean that there exists a being possessed of certain attributes and the atheist denies this, then such a dispute has no place in Heidegger's philosophy and has been superseded. It is significant that he himself is unwilling to be called either theistic or atheistic. The dispute over the existence or non-existence of the substantial God has been left behind with the metaphysical concept of substance itself.

Yet the question is not so simple as to be answered simply by saying that the theism-*versus*-atheism dispute has been overcome. We have seen that Being, as Heidegger conceives it, has divine attributes. Where Being itself can be considered so divine, any additional God has become superfluous. But then, it is possible to conceive Being without divine attributes—Being as alien and oppressive, as in fact Sartre conceives it. The dispute between the theist and the atheist has not so much been overcome as shifted into a new conceptuality. There are still the two possibilities : that Being is divine, worthy of trust and confidence and worship ; or that Being is alien and indifferent. And men will still scan the world, looking for patterns and clues that will support one interpretation or the other. The Heideggerian view, the Sartrean view, the Marxist view, the Freudian view, the Christian view—these all read the character of Being in different ways, and it still makes sense to call some of these ways theistic and some of them atheistic.

Perhaps the theism (and theology) of the future will more and more operate with a conception of God not unlike Heidegger's conception of Being. I do not mean that such conceptions of God will be explicitly derived from Heidegger, but that, as far as their formal structure is concerned, they will have a family resemblance, as it were. Already we have had a powerful exposition of such an idea of God in the philosophical theology of Paul Tillich and have been able to judge from his work something of the possibilities of such an idea of God for expressing and articulating the Christian faith in contemporary terms.

If theism is nowadays to be understood in the manner that I have indicated, then would one say that Heidegger's philosophy is theistic ? Perhaps it is, if he regards Being as the source of meaning and grace. Sartre, on the other hand, would be the true atheist, if he regards Being as devoid of meaning and grace so that man has to create his own meanings and values in an indifferent environment. But clearly there is not just a simple dichotomy between theism and atheism. There seem to be intermediate positions, just as in the past there were various kinds of theism with their corresponding atheisms. Perhaps Heidegger (as he himself would seem to suggest) stands somewhere between the two camps. The Marxist, too, would present an intermediate case ; in so far as he believes in a dialectic of history, he acknowledges an objective ground of meaning in the way things are, and does not accept that Being is absurd or completely amorphous (extreme atheism), yet his own fatalistic belief would hardly qualify as theism. I would myself be unwilling to call Heidegger either a theist or an atheist, and I have mentioned the Marxist to strengthen this point. It seems to me there is little sense in saying (as we sometimes hear it said) that the existentialist or the Marxist is a theist at heart or an anonymous Christian or whatever phrase may be used ; or conversely that a modern theologian like Tillich is really an atheist. Such ways of talking not only blur genuine differences but impugn the integrity of the persons concerned.

I do not think we need be in the least surprised that our discussion of the significance of Heidegger has turned largely on theological questions. A philosophy which sets out from man's quest for Being and ends up by talking of Being's condescension to man is clearly a religious philosophy, however far its concepts may differ from those of traditional metaphysics. I have tried to show elsewhere[63] that Heidegger's ideas provide the framework for the construction of a foundational theology that might carry the weight once placed upon the now

[63] *Principles of Christian Theology* (Scribner, New York : 1966, and SCM Press, London : 1967), p. 39ff.

discredited natural theology. Yet I think one would also have to say that Heidegger's philosophy can stand by itself as an independent system of belief which might be a rival to Christianity. It certainly has affinities to Christian faith, and yet, as already indicated, it has perhaps even closer affinities to Gnosticism. I do not believe, as some people claim, that we are coming into an age of no religion at all. Religion is too much an intrinsic part of what it means to be human for that. But I do wonder whether we are perhaps coming into an age when, among some people at least, private religions will increasingly oust the traditional dogmatic and institutional forms. Heidegger's philosophy could be considered as an attempt to work out a contemporary faith outside of the traditional forms of belief.

In any case, we have to acknowledge this philosophy as one of the most significant attempts in our century to explore and vindicate the spiritual dimensions of human life in face of the threats that confront them.

Glossary

Alienation is the condition of being diverted from the genuine possibilities of existence.

Anxiety is held to be the basic affect, and reveals to the existent his radical finitude.

Authenticity is attained when the existent takes hold of the direction of his own life, whereas in an *inauthentic* existence, this direction is determined for him by external factors.

Being is an ambiguous word in English. When we talk of "a being" or of "the beings", we can mean anything at all that *is:* when we talk of "Being" simply, we mean that character exemplified in all the beings, in virtue of which they *are* and stand out from nothing.

Care is said to be the basic constitution of human existence, and has a threefold structure of possibility, facticity and falling.

Concern is our relation to things (not persons) insofar as this takes such active forms as using, handling, producing, etc.

Everydayness is the routine mode of existence in which we move from one task to the next in accordance with habit and convention.

Existence. This word was traditionally used of anything whatever that is, but in Heidegger and other existentialist writers, the word is restricted to the human existent. This does not imply any unreality on the part of other beings, but draws attention to the fact that the human being stands out (exsists) as the only being that is open to and responsible for what it is. Similarly, the German word *Dasein*, usually left untranslated in English writings, traditionally stood for any kind of existence, but is restricted in Heidegger to the human existent. Of the adjectives derived from "existence", *existential* refers to the universal structures of human existence, while *existentiell* refers to the unique, particular existent.

Facticity denotes all these elements in a human existence that are simply given, not chosen.

Fallenness is the condition of being alienated and scattered.

Ontology is the study of Being. Man is said to be *ontological* because, even if he never explicitly studies Being, he has to decide about his own being in the very act of existing.

Phenomenology is a philosophical method, characterized chiefly by careful analytic description of that which shows itself (the phenomenon).

Possibility, in Heidegger's thought, does not mean just any contingency that may happen, but refers to the open future for which the *Dasein* can decide.

Projecting is the activity by which the *Dasein* throws itself forward into its possibilities.

Significance is acquired by things as they are incorporated into the instrumental world of *Dasein*.

Temporality, with its dimensions of past, present and future, is the most basic characteristic of human existence.

Thrownness is the condition of finding oneself in a world, without knowing where one has come from or where one is going.